ADULT BO

A Life of Grace for the Whole World

A Study Course on the House
of Bishops' Pastoral Teaching on
the Environment

**JERRY CAPPEL and
STEPHANIE M. JOHNSON**

Church Publishing
NEW YORK

Church Publishing
19 East 34th Street
New York, NY 10016
www.churchpublishing.org

Cover design by Jennifer Kopec, 2Pug Design
Typeset by Beth Oberholtzer

Library of Congress Cataloging-in-Publication Data
A record of this book is available from the Library of Congress.

ISBN-13: 978-0-8192-3378-3 (pbk.)
ISBN-13: 978-0-8192-3379-0 (ebook)

Printed in the United States of America

Contents

Welcome and Introduction

The fact that you are reading this suggests that you have an interest in how Christianity intersects with the environmental crisis. You may be a skeptic, a newly open seeker about this issue, or a full-fledged member of the environmental choir. But if this subject interests you at all, you are part of a rising tide. A growing number of people in the church want to explore and understand the connections between present-day environmental realities and core issues of Christian faith, morality, and spirituality.

At the same time, others within the church remain convinced that these issues are largely political and have no place in congregational life. These Christians believe that the church's work should focus solely on the welfare and salvation of human beings, separate from the rest of creation. Environmental issues are viewed as a distraction at best . . . and a political weapon at worst.

This landscape remains complicated, but more and more people within the church are seeking and finding ways to align their faith with the pressing issues of environmental (and human) health and well-being. They are increasingly recognizing that the root causes of environmental exploitation and neglect are often spiritual ones, manifesting in runaway consumerism and unbridled greed. They are also recognizing the links between environmental exploitation and human injustice, and that those who suffer most are often the poor and voiceless among us.

Making these connections is important, for the world needs the church to respond in ways that embody a commitment to love God and neighbor and bear witness to the risen Christ. The world needs from the church not only a helping hand in the work of education and advocacy, but also a Word of God, spoken with confidence and clarity, about the love of God for all creation and our right place in it.

The House of Bishops' Pastoral Teaching on the Environment

In September 2011, the House of Bishops of the Episcopal Church, while meeting in Province IX in Quito, Ecuador, issued a pastoral teaching that challenged the church to face the urgency of the environmental crisis and take faithful action as an expression of our love for God and God's creation. The Episcopal bishops meet twice a year and from time to time (but not often) they produce a pastoral teaching such as this one. This is the first and only time that the House of Bishops has released a pastoral teaching about the environment. This pastoral teaching invites the church to recognize the salvation of *all* creation as the work of Christ in the world. Because we are called to live in Christ and with Christ, we seek to live "a life of grace for the whole world." The pastoral teaching encourages us to address these issues in terms that have always been central to Christian faith and life: repentance, worship, redemption, salvation, obedience, and holiness.

The entire text of the House of Bishops' pastoral teaching is included in the appendix (p. 49). You are encouraged to read it in its entirety in one sitting. At the heart of the pastoral teaching is a call to the church to recognize a real and present challenge of our day:

We are especially called to pay heed to the suffering of the earth. We [human beings] are engaged in the process of destroying our very being. If we cannot live in harmony with the earth, we will not live in harmony with one another.

This is the appointed time for all God's children to work for the common goal of renewing the earth as a hospitable abode for the flourishing of all life. We are called to speak and act on behalf of God's good creation. (paragraphs 4–5)

A Life of Grace for the Whole World

A Life of Grace for the Whole World intends to encourage Christians "to speak and act on behalf of God's good creation." The pastoral teaching reminds us that in so doing, we are also speaking and acting on behalf of God's good church, which is blessed and called as co-workers in God's unfolding plan "to reconcile to himself all things, whether on earth or in heaven, by making peace through the blood of his cross" (Col. 1:20).

The sessions are designed to make connections between the reconciling work of God in the church and the reconciling work of God in all creation. Using the bishops' pastoral teaching, the Bible, and the Episcopal Book of Common Prayer, you will discover important ways that the church can respond faithfully to the mounting social and environmental challenges of our time.

Goals for These Sessions

Each of the five sessions in this book corresponds to a section of the pastoral teaching:

Session 1—A Time for Repentance and Renewal (paragraphs 1–5)
   Goal: *To recognize and respond to the bishops' call for confession, compassion, and attention to the present crisis of the earth; to identify ways to speak and act on behalf of God's good creation*

Session 2—A Time for Grace for the Whole Creation (paragraphs 6–7)
> **Goals:** *To recognize that God's grace and plan for redemption encompass all creation; to commit to embracing the whole creation as fellow recipients of grace*

Session 3—A Time for Justice and Sustainability (paragraphs 8–12)
> **Goals:** *To understand how individual and communal actions can create damaging eco-justice problems that disproportionally affect the poor; to encourage participants to seek to live more just and sustainable lives*

Session 4—A Time to Renew Ancient Practices (paragraphs 13–16)
> **Goals:** *To identify paths for healing through the Church's ancient traditions of fasting, Sabbath-keeping, and mindfulness; to apply these traditions to our individual lives and in our churches*

Session 5—A Time to Commit and Act (paragraphs 17–18)
> **Goal:** *To discern nourishing and effective actions that the participants and their local faith communities can take to respond to the commitments listed by the House of Bishops*

How to Read this Book

This *Adult Booklet* will prepare you for meaningful participation with others in the group sessions. Reading, reflecting, and working with these chapters before each group session will provide you with background and reflection that you can bring to the conversation. We also provide ideas for action following each group session.

Each session includes direct quotes from the pastoral teaching along with reflections and questions to consider. The copy of the pastoral teaching provided in the appendix numbers its paragraphs for easy reference. You will also be invited to explore how the church's prayers and worship—particularly those found in the Episcopal Book of Common Prayer—can help us all experience and express our reconciliation with God and God's creation. We also include opportunities for short Bible-study reflections to help us draw from our biblical heritage.

Before You Begin

Think about your faith journey and your journey regarding environmental issues. List your responses in the table below. In what ways has your Christian faith helped you deepen your commitment? In what ways has your faith been a hindrance?

HELPFUL	HINDRANCE
_____	_____
_____	_____
_____	_____
_____	_____
_____	_____
_____	_____
_____	_____

In these five sessions, your faith will be challenged to become more of a support and help for deepening your care for creation. At the end of the last session, you will have the opportunity to revisit this question, and reflect upon any changes in your answers.

Reading the Pastoral Teaching

In the early church, there were no copy machines or printing presses, and few people could read. A written letter from a beloved leader or another faith community became a precious and celebrated event. Such a letter would be reason for the church to gather to hear it read aloud to the assembly. Paul wrote several of his letters for just this purpose, and they were circulated from church to church and read in each assembly.

The first step to take on this journey is to read the entire pastoral teaching in one sitting. It may enhance your experience to read it aloud, just as it would have been read to a gathered church assembly. As you read it, listen for the challenges it presents to your faith and to the life of the whole church. Listen also for challenges to our lifestyle and choices. You may wish to highlight those sentences in the teaching that stand out to you.

Read the pastoral teaching in one sitting. It is found on page 49 of this book. When done, return here to consider the questions below. As you will discover throughout this *Adult Booklet*, we provide space for you to record your thoughts.

. . . .

Questions to Ponder about **the Pastoral Teaching:**

What is your initial response to the teaching? How comprehensive do you find it? What do you think might be missing? What would you remove or change?

_____

_____

_____

_____

_____

_____

. . . .

SESSION 1
A Time for Repentance and Renewal (Paragraphs 1–5)

Goals

- To recognize and respond to the bishops' call for confession, compassion, and attention to the present crisis of the earth

- To identify ways to speak and act on behalf of God's good creation

From the Bishops' Teaching

[1] We, your bishops, believe these words of Jeremiah describe these times and call us to repentance as we face the unfolding environmental crisis of the earth:

> *How long will the land mourn, and the grass of every field wither? For the wickedness of those who live in it the animals and the birds are swept away, and because people said, "He is blind to our ways." (Jer. 12:4)*

[2] The mounting urgency of our environmental crisis challenges us at this time to confess "our self-indulgent appetites and ways," "our waste and pollution of God's creation," and "our lack of concern for those who come after us" (Ash Wednesday Liturgy, Book of Common Prayer, p. 268). It also challenges us to amend our lives and to work for environmental justice and for more environmentally sustainable practices.

[3] Christians cannot be indifferent to global warming, pollution, natural resource depletion, species extinctions, and habitat destruction, all of which threaten life on our planet. Because so many of these threats are driven by greed, we must also actively seek to create more compassionate and sustainable economies that support the well-being of all God's creation.

[4] We are especially called to pay heed to the suffering of the earth. The Anglican Communion Environmental Network calls to mind the dire consequences our environment faces: "We know that . . . we are now demanding more than [the earth] is able to provide. Science confirms what we already know: our human footprint is changing the face of the earth and because we come from the earth, it is changing us too. We are engaged in the process of destroying our very being. If we cannot live in harmony with the earth, we will not live in harmony with one another."

[5] This is the appointed time for all God's children to work for the common goal of renewing the earth as a hospitable abode for the flourishing of all life. We are called to speak and act on behalf of God's good creation.

—The Pastoral Teaching (paragraphs 1–5)

Before the Session: Graceful Intentions

Science confirms what we already know: our human footprint is changing the face of the earth and because we come from the earth, it is changing us too.

In 2011, author and environmental activist Bill McKibben published a new book with the title, *Eaarth: Making a Life on a Tough New Planet*. The spelling in the title was not a typo. McKibben deliberately changed the spelling of *Earth* to *Eaarth* to illustrate the point of the book: human activity has already altered the living systems of planet earth to such an extent that the planet is fast becoming a different place; it is less hospitable to human thriving and to the ongoing existence of countless other creatures. Future generations will have to adapt to living on a planet that is very different than the one upon which we were born.

This means that the church is living, worshipping, serving, and proclaiming in a world in many ways unlike the one inhabited by earlier generations. We face many converging trends, from climate disruption to deforestation and species extinction, from toxins and pollution to a growing scarcity of fresh water and arable land. All of these trends, along with a growing worldwide population, have together altered the earth in fundamental and sometimes irrevocable ways.

. . . .

Questions to Ponder about **Our Planet:**

Do you agree with Bill McKibben's conclusion that human activity on the planet has already made it a different place? What in your experience confirms or contradicts it?

_____

_____

_____

_____

_____

. . . .

Given the new reality in which we find ourselves, the church needs to revisit its inherited faith and practice. How do we apply our values and teachings in the midst of this unprecedented situation? The language, priorities, and practices of our parents and grandparents cannot function unaltered in the context of an altered earth.

In other words, the faith of the past generations that made sense on planet earth may need to adjust to become the faith for future generations who live on planet *Eaarth*.

Of course, the church has always been making adjustments to its faith and practice. In response to big social changes such as war, women's suffrage, civil rights, and other movements, the church continues to make changes to its priorities, policies, and practices. As the church has in the past, we are called to reengage and reimagine Christian faith for our own day.

Questions to Ponder about **Social Change:**

Have you been witness to or been involved in large social changes in the past or present? What were the issues? What kinds of challenge did they present to your faith? What kinds of change do they continue to demand from the church?

_____

_____

_____

_____

_____

The pastoral teaching acknowledges this reality:

Christians cannot be indifferent to global warming, pollution, natural resource depletion, species extinctions, and habitat destruction, all of which threaten life on our planet. Because so many of these threats are driven by greed, we must also actively seek to create more compassionate and sustainable economies that support the well-being of all God's creation. We are especially called to pay heed to the suffering of the earth.

In many ways, these are new challenges presented to the church, and they challenge the church to reconsider its role as both participant in the problems and actor in the solutions. Greed, of course, is nothing new, and acts of compassion have always been hallmarks of a faithful life in Christ. But what is new for human societies today is that the consequences of our choices have unparalleled consequences for the whole web of life. Continuing with business as usual is already causing great suffering worldwide and could inflict unspeakable harm in the very near future.

Larry Rasmussen uses a biblical metaphor to capture this essential idea:

> Our present condition is new wine without new wineskins. This does not bode well ... The new wine is not the vintage we expected. It is a planet undergoing sufficient change in its core surface processes that it tallies as geophysical, and not only economic, political, cultural, or religious, change; change of such an order of magnitude that some scientists have named it a new geological age.[1]

The impact of our species on the planet in just a few hundred years is comparable to the changes wrought in geologic time over hundreds of thousands of years. While the planet has undergone such extensive changes before, it has never experienced them in such a short span of time. This is something new on the earth, and something new set before the church as a challenge to its faith and practice.

We all need to recognize the relevance of these issues to the life of the church today and to invite new forms of repentance and renewal

---

1. Larry Rasmussen, in an address at the *Festival of Faiths* in Louisville, KY, Nov. 2010.

that connect to these realities. As Christians, how are we to live in this new age? What does the gospel of God's salvation say to us in this day? What does it call us to say to others about these things?

. . . .

Questions to Ponder about **Repentance:**

How open is your faith community to entering into "new forms of repentance and renewal"? What are some potential opportunities for repentance and renewal in your faith community?

_____

_____

_____

_____

_____

. . . .

Questions to Ponder about **Your Own "Graceful Intentions":**

What changes in your own life of faith, prayer, and behavior have you made that are ways to "speak and act on behalf of God's good creation"? What further changes might you consider?

_____

_____

_____

_____

_____

_____

_____

What changes in your faith community have been made
to "speak and act on behalf of God's good creation"? What
further changes might be considered?

_____

_____

_____

_____

_____

_____

Take a walk through your living spaces, and as you walk, ask,
"How does this space speak and act on behalf of God's good
creation? In what ways does it speak against it?" What changes
could be made? What changes seem impossible or impractical?

_____

_____

_____

_____

_____

_____

_____

After the Session: Graceful Living

One option during the group session was to read and discuss Jeremiah 12:4, where the prophet Jeremiah recognizes that the land mourns and the grass withers. Can you think of times and places where you have witnessed that the land was mourning and the grass was withered? As you go about your day and the week to come, prepare to take an inventory of times and places where you see that the land is mourning around you, and that the grass has withered. Where are such places? What are the root causes of this phenomena?

A second option during the group session was to reconsider the Ash Wednesday Litany of Penitence in light of our present-day environmental crisis. As you go about your day-to-day business, notice the times of opportunity for confession of things done or left undone as it concerns the environmental crisis. Create a list of items that could be added to a confession, and plan a time to make that confession sometime this week.

Consider the land, air, and water you will encounter during the week. Determine ahead of time to take an action on behalf of creation if the opportunity presents itself. Be alert for things done or left undone. Turn off wasted water, pick up trash, and turn off unneeded lights. Lighten your footprint by avoiding wasteful packaging and unnecessary driving. Be aware of the impact of the food you eat. Reduce, reuse, and recycle.

SESSION 2

A Time for Grace for the Whole World (Paragraphs 6–7)

Goals

- To recognize that God's grace and plan for redemption encompasses the whole world
- To embrace the whole world as fellow recipients of grace

From the Bishops' Teaching

[6] Looking back to the creation accounts in Genesis, we see God's creation was "very good," providing all that humans would need for abundant, peaceful life. In creating the world God's loving concern extended to the whole of it, not just to humans. And the scope of God's redemptive love in Christ is equally broad: The Word became incarnate in Christ not just for our sake, but for the salvation of the whole world. In the book of Revelation we read that God will restore the goodness and completeness of creation in the "New Jerusalem." Within this new city, God renews and redeems the natural world rather than obliterating it. We now live in that time between God's creation of this good world and its

final redemption: "The whole creation has been groaning in labor pains until now; and not only the creation, but we ourselves, who have the first fruits of the Spirit, groan inwardly while we wait for . . . the redemption of our bodies" (Rom. 8:22–3).

[7] Affirming the biblical witness to God's abiding and all-encompassing love for creation, we recognize that we cannot separate ourselves as humans from the rest of the created order. The creation story itself presents the interdependence of all God's creatures in their wonderful diversity and fragility, and in their need of protection from dangers of many kinds. This is why the church prays regularly for the peace of the whole world, for seasonable weather and an abundance of the fruits of the earth, for a just sharing of resources, and for the safety of all who suffer. This includes our partner creatures: animals, birds, and fish who are being killed or made sick by the long-term effects of deforestation, oil spills, and a host of other ways in which we intentionally and unintentionally destroy or poison their habitat.

—The Pastoral Teaching (paragraphs 6–7)

Before the Session: Graceful Intentions

In the end, we will protect only what we love. We will love only what we understand. We will understand only what we are taught.

—Baba Dioum

These words from the Senegalese environmentalist Baba Dioum succinctly describe the goal of this section of the teaching—to recognize that God's love and purpose encompasses all creation and to join in that love. The corollary to these words would be:

We will not save what we do not love, and we cannot love what we do not know.

So, the heart of the work of embracing grace for all creation is to "familiarize ourselves" (make family) not just with our human kin, but also with the whole family of God's created order. For that, the church will need to invite God's good creation more fully into its liturgy, prayer, and fellowship, which are the places where the church learns how to recognize each other and be family.

This could be called sacramental work. A sacrament is often defined as "an outward and visible sign of inward and spiritual divine grace." Christian baptism is a sacrament, in that the visible presence of water points to the underlying presence of God's work of salvation in Christ in the life of the baptized. The pastoral teaching calls us to recognize how the saving work of God is also present in the entire web of life and the planet itself:

> The Word became incarnate in Christ not just for our sake, but for the salvation of the whole world.
>
> —The Pastoral Teaching (paragraph 6)

What outward and visible signs might help the church recognize the inward and spiritual divine grace at work on behalf of the whole earth? What would help the church to expand its understanding of family to include the entire earth-community?

Perhaps the first step is to identify the places where the church traditionally celebrates love and family. When does the church most feel like a family? Is it in excellent worship? Good fellowship? Shared service? Where are words of love and appreciation commonly spoken? During the peace? At potlucks? How is grace and salvation most openly recognized and celebrated? In church music? In the Eucharist? In the presence of children? These are the times and places that make church life together become *sacred* life together. The challenge presented in the pastoral teaching is this: How can the church expand its sacred community to more fully encompass our nonhuman kin?

Questions to Ponder about **Celebration:**

What are the celebrations of fellowship in our faith community? Where do we celebrate each other and recognize each other as family? How within these might we include the larger creation?

_____

_____

_____

_____

_____

_____

> Affirming the biblical witness to God's abiding and all-encompassing love for creation, we recognize that we cannot separate ourselves as humans from the rest of the created order.
>
> —The Pastoral Teaching (paragraph 7)

But we do separate ourselves if, in our acts of worship and fellowship, we include only human concerns and recognize only human salvation. We separate ourselves if, while being thoughtful and careful with each person present, we are then thoughtless and careless with how we behave toward the rest of creation. In our day, it perpetuates that separation to enjoy our human fellowship while thoughtlessly wasting water and food, polluting our surroundings, and sending to our landfills the waste of our convenience. It is important to recognize that such thoughtless and careless behaviors are not simply poor stewardship. They are also violations of fellowship and God's abiding and all-encompassing love for creation. It is not only that they contribute to human injustice; they also dishonor the work of the incarnate Christ to save not just human beings, but the whole world.

. . . .

Questions to Ponder about **Separations:**

What choices and actions can you identify in your own life that separate you from the rest of the created order? What choices can you identify in your faith community?

_____

_____

_____

_____

_____

_____

. . . .

The implications of this understanding of God's work in the world are deep and wide. If the flourishing of creation is a sign of God's unfolding reconciliation of all things in Christ, then our waste and pollution of the world is violation of our gospel witness. If God's work in the world is to save it, then our destruction of the world is not only human foolishness; it is a failure of fellowship with both God and creation. This points to the deep spiritual work within this challenge from the pastoral teaching.

Our need is to recognize the salvation of *all* creation as the work of Christ in the world and to include it in our very work of *being* Christ in the world. As Archbishop Desmond Tutu has said, "The act of reconciling us to all of God's creation is Christ's supreme work."

This deep work of recognition cannot be accomplished through occasional lessons for children or annual celebrations in honor of St. Francis. This kind of transformation must engage the daily and weekly life of the church. The church is being challenged to more fully include in its worship, prayer, fellowship, and service the proclamation of Christ's redemption and reconciliation of all things.

If it is true that we will save only what we love, the converse is also true: we will be saved only by what we love. By inviting the rest of creation into our worship, prayer, and life together, we in turn will learn to love all aspects of creation and to recognize their holiness and worth. As we acknowledge their holiness, we will more fully recognize the holiness of all things, including our own lives.

. . . .

Questions to Ponder about **Your Own "Graceful Intentions":**

What changes could you make in your habits and choices that would deepen your fellowship with the whole creation?

_____

_____

_____

_____

_____

What next steps might your faith community make to more consistently and fully recognize its fellowship with the whole creation?

_____

_____

_____

_____

_____

_____

_____

What changes could you make to your prayers to more fully
include the larger web of life in them? Write down some
changes or additions to prayers you routinely say that would
acknowledge your fellowship with all creation.

_____

_____

_____

_____

_____

_____

Select a favorite song that reminds you of your joy and appreciation for creation. Each day, select a time to play the song as
you look around or walk around, rejoicing in and with creation.

. . . .

After the Session: Graceful Living

During the group session, you may have been challenged to create
a way to describe the Bible story of salvation to either a person for
whom English was a second language (option 1), or for a six-year-

old (option 2). The group was invited to consider what the Bible teaches about the role of creation in salvation as described in Genesis 1, Romans 8, and Revelation 21. Read again Romans 8:22–23 and Revelation 21:2. Take a few moments to imagine how the fulfillment of these visions for God's salvation might look in your neighborhood. Draw a picture, write a poem, or make of list of the features of this scene as envisioned in these texts.

As you go about your week, look for ways to join in God's work of redemption of all creation. Spread kindness and healing to all living things as you go about your day. Reduce suffering as best you can, and restore a healthy and natural balance wherever you can.

SESSION 3

A Time for Justice and Sustainability (paragraphs 8–12)

Goals

- To understand how individual and communal actions can create damaging eco-justice problems that disproportionally affect the poor
- To encourage participants to seek to live more just and sustainable lives

From the Bishops' Teaching

[8] One of the most dangerous and daunting challenges we face is global climate change. This is, at least in part, a direct result of our burning of fossil fuels. Such human activities could raise worldwide average temperatures by three to eleven degrees Fahrenheit in this century. Rising average temperatures are already wreaking environmental havoc, and, if unchecked, portend devastating consequences for every aspect of life on earth.

[9] The church has always had as one of its priorities a concern for the poor and the suffering. Therefore, we need not agree on the

fundamental causes of human devastation of the environment, or on what standard of living will allow sustainable development, or on the roots of poverty in any particular culture, in order to work to minimize the impact of climate change. It is the poor and the disadvantaged who suffer most from callous environmental irresponsibility. Poverty is both a local and a global reality. A healthy economy depends absolutely on a healthy environment.

[10] The wealthier nations whose industries have exploited the environment, and who are now calling for developing nations to reduce their impact on the environment, seem to have forgotten that those who consume most of the world's resources also have contributed the most pollution to the world's rivers and oceans, have stripped the world's forests of healing trees, have destroyed both numerous species and their habitats, and have added the most poison to the earth's atmosphere. We cannot avoid the conclusion that our irresponsible industrial production and consumption-driven economy lie at the heart of the current environmental crisis.

[11] Privileged Christians in our present global context need to move from a culture of consumerism to a culture of conservation and sharing. The challenge is to examine one's own participation in ecologically destructive habits. Our churches must become places where we have honest debates about, and are encouraged to live into, more sustainable ways of living. God calls us to die to old ways of thinking and living and be raised to new life with renewed hearts and minds.

[12] Although many issues divide us as people of faith, unprecedented ecumenical and interfaith cooperation is engaging the concern to protect our planet. And yet, efforts to stop environmental degradation must not be simply imposed from above. Those most affected must have a hand in shaping decisions. For example, we welcome efforts in the United States to involve Native American

tribal leaders and to empower local community organizations to address environmental issues. Similar strategies need to be employed in myriad communities in various locales.

—The Pastoral Teaching (paragraphs 8–12)

Before the Session: Graceful Intentions

The Christian church has a long tradition of social justice. While its application may vary from group to group, most churches accept some level of obligation to recognize and respond to issues of injustice with both individuals and in society. The pastoral teaching acknowledges this fact in paragraph nine:

> The church has always had as one of its priorities a concern for the poor and the suffering.

This priority is woven directly into the baptismal covenant, in promises made not only at each baptism, but also with each renewal of baptismal vows made by the whole church throughout the year (Book of Common Prayer, p. 94):

> *Celebrant:* Will you seek and serve Christ in all persons, loving your neighbor as yourself?
> *People:* I will, with God's help.
> *Celebrant:* Will you strive for justice and peace among all people, and respect the dignity of every human being?
> *People:* I will, with God's help.

Of course, what striving for justice and peace is and the obligations it places upon each us is where the debate begins. The age-old question posed in the gospels as a challenge to Jesus still lives among us today—"Who is my neighbor?" That question challenges the promises of the Baptismal Covenant as well. Who and what is included in this pledge to serve, love, and respect? Every human being, certainly. But every living thing as well? And does such service, love, and respect extend to the stars, mountains, and the living streams that also praise God?

And how far does our neighborhood extend? If pollution or destruction supported by our choices eventually leads to the impoverishment or displacement of distant people or creatures, does that become our issue of justice and peace here at home? And if I personally benefit from that pollution or destruction by cheaper prices or easier access, am I then taking part in the pollution and destruction as well?

Making the connections of justice between our personal buying habits and their impacts on fishermen or subsistence farmers half way around the world is a real challenge. Choosing to modify or limit our lifestyles for the sake of a distant good does not come easily to us. Frugality and financial responsibility must increasingly be moderated by environmental considerations. Resisting the temptation to buy the cheapest goods because of the innate injustice in the way they were produced is a new behavior to most of us. Making the connections between these choices and our faith is also new to us.

. . . .

Questions to Ponder about **Injustice:**

Look around the place where you are right now. What links can you make between your surroundings and potential injustices elsewhere in the world? What human communities are being impacted? What nonhuman ones?

_____

_____

_____

_____

_____

_____

_____

_____

. . . .

The key topic explored in these paragraphs is "eco-justice." The World Council of Churches describes eco-justice as linking environmental justice and social justice so that we address both humanity's destruction of the earth *and* the abuse of economic and political power that cause the poor to suffer disproportionately from the effects of environmental damage.

The pastoral teaching names climate change as one of the most daunting examples of this. It is daunting because of the size and complexity of the issues involved—both scientific and economic—and the impact it has on our lives.

The teaching also names other "various pollutions" and practices, and links them to our "irresponsible industrial production and consumption-driven economy." Making these links and comprehending the import of them makes eco-justice perhaps the most controversial and complex concept for us to engage as a community of faith. The teaching drives to the heart of the matter when it names wealth, privilege, and a consumer-driven economy as key contributors to eco-injustice. If these lie at the heart of these challenges, then the challenge is a spiritual and moral one, and are connected to our faith.

Questions to Ponder about **Industrial Production:**

Look around at your surroundings again. What economic forces are implicated as "irresponsible industrial production"? What changes would have to be made to "strive for justice and peace"?

_____

_____

_____

_____

_____

_____

This concept of eco-justice encourages people of faith to consider the impacts our choices have on the environment and its communities. The pastoral teaching presents three particular challenges to deepen our engagement with eco-justice:

Make connections between climate change and poverty (paragraphs 8–9). The first challenge is to make the connections between climate change and its impact on issues of economic justice. While American society is slowly waking up to climate change and its resulting super storms or extended droughts, there is yet very little recognition of its connections to economic impacts all around the world. Melting ice caps, altered seasons, warming oceans, and extended ranges of plants and insects all have enormous economic impacts as the changes upturn long-established patterns and habitats.

Make connections between our consumerist lifestyle, the dependence of the economy on the status quo, and the environmental impacts of it (paragraphs 10–11). A second challenge is to make the connections between our own personal participation in a consumer-driven economy and the impacts on issues of justice. To make these connections, Christians will need to learn how to consider more than price and quality of items they buy, but also where, how, and by whom it was made . . . and the impact on each. Further, Christians will need to deepen their understanding of not only their local economy but also the economies of places where their own goods and services originated.

Expand your community of engagement (paragraph 12). A third challenge is to enlarge our communities of partnership and fellowship. We are challenged to recognize and engage a larger, worldwide neighborhood of concern as we discover our common cause.

These issues are complicated in their science, economics, and politics, and coming to a sophisticated understanding of all the facts is not within reach of each of us. But the challenge to the quality of our Christian faith and the compassion and godliness it calls from us is something each one of us can grasp. These challenges from the pastoral teaching call for the hard work of listening with openness and grace to those who challenge us with these issues, to look with willing and compassionate eyes to the suffering of others, and to consider with repentant hearts our role in the problems. It is this call to an open heart, ears, and mind that is clearly called for by our faith. As your group meets to study and discuss these difficult issues, look for opportunities to focus upon faith, compassion, and repentance, and avoid being distracted by economic and political debates.

The pastoral teaching offers an opportunity to consider how our society's corporate and institutional systems—combined with individual lifestyle choices—affect the environment, and how "privileged Christians" are called to respond to these harmful impacts with honest reflection and conversion (paragraph 8). As the pastoral teaching clearly asks for honest debate and reflection on how our values mesh with our spiritual calling, this section of the teaching calls us to deepen our appreciation of what it means to follow Jesus and to be stewards and guardians of God's creation.

. . . .

Questions to Ponder about **Your Own "Graceful Intentions":**

A well-known adage in peace and justice activist circles is "No peace without justice." Applications of this are recognizable in areas of war and conflict. But how might it also apply to environmental issues? What are some local issues of unrest and conflict that have environmental injustice as a root cause?

_____

_____

_____

_____

_____

_____

The bishops call us to move "from a culture of consumerism to a culture of conservation and sharing" as a necessary change Christians must undergo. What links can you name between environmental injustices in your community and an established "culture of consumerism"? What would it take to make the necessary changes to enhance a "culture of sharing"?

_____

_____

_____

_____

_____

_____

· ·

After the Session: Graceful Living

Option 1: Exodus 23:10–12. If your group used this option, you had a conversation about the role of Sabbath rest for the land and animals. As you go about your life this week, in what ways can you grant Sabbath to other people and to living things this week? In what ways can you take it upon yourself?

Option 2: The Baptismal Covenant. If your group used this option, you had a conversation about the Baptismal Covenant and its application to environmental issues. As you go about your life this week, in what ways can you strive for peace with the people and places you encounter this week? In what ways can you strive for justice?

Take up the bishops' challenge "to examine one's own participation in ecologically destructive habits." Commit yourself to a moment of daily prayer this week, and dedicate the prayer time to naming ways you have noticed being caught up in "a culture of consumerism" that day. Repent as best you can and pray for the grace to live gracefully.

Gather your receipts, bills, statements, or other forms of listing how you have participated in buying and selling over the past few weeks. Prayerfully consider how each item bought or sold was a form of participation in forms of justice or injustice. How might you move closer to living in justice and peace?

A Time to Renew Ancient Practices (Paragraphs 13–16)

Goals

- To identify paths for healing through the church's ancient traditions of fasting, Sabbath-keeping, and mindfulness
- To apply these traditions to our individual lives and in our churches

From the Bishops' Teaching

[13] Our current environmental challenges call us to ongoing forms of repentance: we must turn ourselves around, and come to think, feel, and act in new ways. Ancient wisdom and spiritual disciplines from our faith offer deep resources to help address this environmental crisis. Time-honored practices of fasting, Sabbath-keeping, and Christ-centered mindfulness bear particular promise for our time.

[14] Fasting disciplines and heals our wayward desires and appetites, calling us to balance our individual needs with God's will for the whole world. In fasting we recognize that human hungers require more than filling the belly. In God alone are our desires finally

fulfilled. Commended in the Book of Common Prayer, fasting is grounded in the practices of Israel, taught by Jesus, and sustained in Christian tradition. The ecological crisis extends and deepens the significance of such fasting as a form of self-denial: those who consume more than their fair share must learn to exercise self-restraint so that the whole community of creation might be sustained.

[15] Sabbath-keeping is rooted in the book of Genesis, where the seventh day is the day in which God, humans, and the rest of creation are in right relationship. In our broken world, keeping the Sabbath is a way of remembering and anticipating that world for which God created us. Sabbath requires rest, that we might remember our rightful place as God's creatures in relationship with every other creature of God. Such rest implicitly requires humans to live lightly on the face of the earth, neither to expend energy nor to consume it, not to work for gain alone, but to savor the grace and givenness of creation.

[16] The practice of Christ-centered mindfulness, that is, the habitual recollection of Christ, calls believers to a deepened awareness of the presence of God in their own lives, in other people, and in every aspect of the world around us. Such spiritual perception should make faithful people alert to the harmful effects of our lifestyles, attentive to our carbon footprint and to the dangers of overconsumption. It should make us profoundly aware of the gift of life and less prone to be ecologically irresponsible in our consumption and acquisition.

—The Pastoral Teaching (paragraphs 13–16)

Before the Session: Graceful Intentions

In the pastoral teaching we read:

Ancient wisdom and spiritual disciplines from our faith offer deep resources to help address this environmental crisis. Time-honored practices of fasting, Sabbath-keeping, and Christ-centered mindfulness bear particular promise for our time.

In these paragraphs of the teaching we are challenged to consider the promising resources of some long-established Christian spiritual practices for our own day and time. The bishops make a clear connection between the environmental ills manifest in the world, the condition of our souls, and how helpful practices such as fasting, Sabbath, and mindfulness could be. We are challenged to make these connections for ourselves.

But most people do not recognize the long and established history of these practices in the church nor have a good understanding of how these practices contribute to Christian godliness. For the average church member, fasting and contemplation are reserved for religious superstars. Honoring the Sabbath is little more than Sunday church-going. And few make connections between these traditional practices and our current environmental challenges.

What are these connections? Why do the bishops say that these practices bear "particular promise for our time"? How do they help us to "turn ourselves around, and come to think, feel, and act in new ways"? Making these connections between our actions and their spiritual roots is placed as a challenge before us. Making them between soul healing and environmental healing is at the heart of this section of the teaching.

· ·

Questions to Ponder about **Habits:**

What is it about "our time" that particularly calls for the renewal of the holy habits recommended by the bishops? What "bad habits" can you think of that might be healed by the "good habits" of Sabbath-keeping, mindfulness, and fasting?

Fasting is a practice viewed by many as something reserved for past ages or special Christians, and not as a common practice for many in the church today. Or, we have reduced the fasting practices of the past to fish on Fridays and giving up chocolate in Lent. And if practiced at all, we view the act as simply an act of penitence or obligation rather than an exercise of personal discipline. But these small acknowledgments of the church year are not what the bishops have identified as the practice that can lead us to balance our needs with that of the whole world.

The purpose of fasting mentioned in the pastoral teaching is to expand our recognition of spiritual hunger and enlarge our capacity for self-restraint. While there are many good reasons to practice fasting, the goal identified from the pastoral teaching is to connect the practice of fasting to the goal of finding a more appropriate life balance within the whole of God's creation so that life can flourish for all. The spiritual result of such a discipline is to become more content with what we have and more empowered to consume less, so our consumption will not limit sustenance for others. Armed with such contentment, we are free from the need to constantly strive and work, consume and collect.

To practice fasting is to exercise mastery of the self, not slavery of the self. To practice fasting is to practice the power of choosing how we will live in the world, and to align our lifestyles with the well-being of all living things. To practice fasting is to exercise the freedom to say yes or no to the constant demands of body and society. If what we consume becomes an issue of injustice, the practice of fasting helps us to walk away. If expectations of society lead to toxicity of body or soul, the practice of fasting helps us to choose better alternatives.

. . . .

Questions to Ponder about **Fasting:**

What methods of fasting might help you to enhance your recognition of spiritual hunger and enlarge your capacity for self-restraint? From what things could you fast to take this journey?

_____

_____

_____

_____

_____

_____

. . . .

Perhaps of special importance for the environmental challenges of our day is the practice of the Sabbath. The pastoral teaching suggests that Sabbath is a universal principle anchored in the very act of creation and an urgent truth we need to recover in our day. The culmination of the creation stories in Genesis was not the creation of humans on the sixth day, so that we might begin our project of owning and dominating all things. Rather, it was the seventh day, the day of rest, so that all might find rest in the goodness of

God. Sabbath is not simply a covenant marker for Israel nor a day of rest and worship for Christians, but a core principle of justice and right relationship rooted in creation itself, reaffirmed by Jesus in his ministry, and culminated in the final act of reconciliation to God through Christ of creation.

At the heart of Sabbath-keeping is the recognition that our life (and all life in creation) does not rely solely upon our own work, but also upon God's provision. It is also the recognition that the value of creation is not measured solely in utilitarian terms, but also as beloved creatures of the God who grants Sabbath rest. In living out that recognition, we become free from the endless need to work and grasp and collect in the effort to establish and secure our lives. We are free to rest, because God is a god of Sabbath rest.

Sabbath-keeping is not a burden of the pious nor a test of obedience. It is the privilege of the cared-for and the practice of freedom. The enjoyment of Sabbath is the joy of those who are rich in grace and not bound the idols and false loyalties that demand endless work and striving. The abundant grace given at creation is the freely given grace of God so that all aspects of God's creation are fellow participants in Sabbath rest. When God rested on the seventh day, so did God's creation. This truth was established in the law of Israel, which not only kept Sabbath as the people of God, but also *granted* Sabbath to the alien, the animals, and the land itself.

The grace of Sabbath was also made clear by Jesus, who condemned lives of grasping acquisition and challenged the hierarchies of power and exploitation. That grace is also expressed in the Sermon on the Mount (Matthew 5), where Jesus invites each to consider the birds and the flowers, understand the provision of God, and put down their anxious thoughts about tomorrow. The practice of Sabbath offers a path of discipleship with Jesus, who taught us to pray for *daily* bread. Sabbath keeping, at its heart, is rest and contentment—not because we have to, but because we are free to.

In this practice we are moved to recognize how our rampant consumption and the consequent exhaustion of living systems are a violation of God's Sabbath rest in creation. To practice Sabbath is to declare that God continues to care for all living things, that God's kingdom has drawn near, and that all creation benefits from it. Sabbath offers an alternative story to the "American Dream" story, which centers on work and acquisition. It offers a path to empowerment through trust and contentment rather than struggle and competition. It offers a path of discernment for choosing what is wise and a prophetic voice about these core issues of our day.

. . . .

Questions to Ponder about **Contentment:**

What are some places in your life that are driven by a struggle for security? What are some places where your faith community fosters anxiety and discontent, rather than peace and contentment? What are the spiritual roots of these struggles and anxieties?

_____

_____

_____

_____

_____

. . . .

Christian mindfulness is to the mind what fasting is to the body. Just as fasting nurtures freedom from the body's impulses and desires, so mindfulness nurtures freedom from the impulses of the mind. Just as fasting can serve to awaken us to the physical hungers and driving appetites within and around us, so mindfulness can serve to awaken us to the spiritual loneliness and mental restlessness within and around us.

Every time and place is a time and place of prayer.

—Catherine of Siena, *The Dialogue*[2]

This truth has been understood by the church from its foundation. However, the challenge in our day is to add to this understanding the connections between these restless impulses and the environmental crisis. The same spiritual malaise that fuels our society's willingness to build today at the expense of tomorrow lies behind each individual's willingness to uncritically participate in such misjudgment. What lies behind our willingness to "soil our own beds" with our practices of production and consumption has a spiritual component that must be recognized and addressed. The bishops call this out in their teaching, and place their finger on this urgent spiritual need of our day: a deepened awareness of the presence of God in our lives, in other people, and in every aspect of the world around us.

A deeper awareness of the presence of God in our own lives can serve to ease the grip of anxiety and insecurity that fuels our willingness to consume at levels harmful to others. A deeper awareness of God in other people can serve to strengthen our compassion for those harmed by exploitation and shortsightedness. And a deeper awareness of the presence of God in every aspect of the world around us can awaken us to the deep sinfulness of diminishing and destroying the creation God loves. Such awareness, born and nurtured by the practice of Christian mindfulness, is an essential component of the repentance and renewal being called forth by the groaning of creation.

---

2. *Catherine of Siena: The Dialogue,* trans. Suzanne Noffke, O. P. (New York: Paulist Press, 1980), 145.

Questions to Ponder about **Making Purchases:**

What were your motives for making your most recent purchases? How aware are you of the "ecological footprint" of those items?

_____

_____

_____

_____

_____

_____

Questions to Ponder about **Your Own "Graceful Intentions":**

Of the three disciplines recommended by the bishops, which one speaks most clearly to you? Begin now to add a convenient and simple form of practicing that discipline. (Beginning with simplicity and convenience is an important strategy in improving our ability to sustain the practice.)

_____

_____

_____

_____

_____

_____

Take a walk into one your favorite outdoor places of peace and ho-liness. While on that walk, find a small stone, nut, or item that speaks to you of God's presence in some way. Carry the item with you for the next several days, taking it out from time to time, and ask the ques-tion, "How have I been discontent or anxious in the past few hours?" Breathe a prayer of trust and forgiveness, and carry on with your day.

After the Session: Graceful Living

In the coming week, look for opportunities to take some Sabbath rest from work and consuming. Also look for opportunities to grant Sabbath rest to other people, places, or creatures. In what ways will you allow the recognition of God's Sabbath to change how you will use your time and energy?

Identify two to three opportunities to practice mindfulness in the coming week, and set reminders to practice them. Such oppor-tunities might include:

- Take a "mindful walk" of thankfulness and praise, in which you give thanks for as many creatures and living things as you can. An alternative is a mindful walk of confession and intercession, where you pray for the places of degradation, pollution, and misuse that you witness as you walk.

- Eat a "mindful meal" where you consider the path each food item has taken to reach your plate, giving thanks for its provision and confessing any complicity in its unnecessary suffering.

- Fasting can include many things of heart, mind, and body. Con-sider undertaking a fast of something that creates anxiety, dis-content, or distraction for you. Such things might be caffeine, television, or your cellphone. You could also fast from habits such as complaining or multi-tasking. Identify one for you and commit to a reasonable fast with a clear beginning and ending point.

SESSION 5

A Time to Commit and Act (Paragraphs 17–18)

Goal

- To discern nourishing and effective actions that the participants and their local faith communities can take to respond to the commitments listed by the House of Bishops

From the Bishops' Teaching

[17] In assuming with new vigor our teaching office, we, your bishops, commit ourselves to a renewal of these spiritual practices in our own lives, and invite you to join us in this commitment for the good of our souls and the life of the world. Moreover, in order to honor the goodness and sacredness of God's creation, we, as brothers and sisters in Christ, commit ourselves and urge every Episcopalian:

- To acknowledge the urgency of the planetary crisis in which we find ourselves, and to repent of any and all acts of greed, over-consumption, and waste that have contributed to it;

- To lift up prayers in personal and public worship for environmental justice, for sustainable development, and for help in restoring right relations both among humankind and between humankind and the rest of creation;

- To take steps in our individual lives, and in community, public policy, business, and other forms of corporate decision-making, to practice environmental stewardship and justice, including (1) a commitment to energy conservation and the use of clean, renewable sources of energy; and (2) efforts to reduce, reuse, and recycle, and whenever possible to buy products made from recycled materials;

- To seek to understand and uproot the political, social, and economic causes of environmental destruction and abuse;

- To advocate for a "fair, ambitious, and binding" climate treaty, and to work toward climate justice through reducing our own carbon footprint and advocating for those most negatively affected by climate change.

[18] May God give us the grace to heed the warnings of Jeremiah and to accept the gracious invitation of the incarnate Word to live, in, with, and through him, a life of grace for the whole world, that thereby all the earth may be restored and humanity filled with hope. Rejoicing in your works, O Lord, send us forth with your Spirit to renew the face of the earth, that the world may once again be filled with your good things: the trees watered abundantly, springs rushing between the hills in verdant valleys, all the earth made fruitful, your manifold creatures, birds, beasts, and humans, all quenching their thirst and receiving their nourishment from you once again in due season (Ps. 104).

—The Pastoral Teaching (paragraphs 17–18)

Before the Session: Graceful Intentions

In this final section of the pastoral teaching, the bishops commit to turning their conviction into action and invite us to follow. They also provide us an opportunity to discern what specific actions can heal creation and strengthen our own faith. The list of actions includes personal repentance, prayer, and worship, advocacy for eco-justice, and responses to climate change. This invites a whole-person, whole-community response. It challenges us to get involved in heart and hand, soul and strength. It challenges both church and society. The breadth of this challenge is important, for these issues run deeper than science, politics, and economics. They are also issues of faith and right relationship to God. Heart, mind, soul, and strength are rightly called forth from us.

This recognizes both the breadth and the depth of the issues before us. After decades of activism, politics, and scientific studies, the world's societies are barely waking up to the needed changes, and the Christian church is no further along than society in general. The late Thomas Berry, a Catholic priest, historian, and eco-theologian, clearly defined the problem:

> In our present attitude the natural world remains a commodity to be bought and sold, not a sacred reality to be venerated. The deep psychic shift needed to withdraw us from the fascination of the industrial world and the deceptive gifts that it gives us is too difficult for simply the avoidance of its difficulties or the attractions of its benefits. Eventually, only our sense of the sacred will save us.[3]

It is this work of recognizing and practicing our "sense of the sacred" that demands from us the full range of repentance, prayer, and realignment of our lives called for in the pastoral teaching. Our

---

3. Thomas Berry, in the foreword to Thomas Merton, *When the Trees Say Nothing*, ed. Kathleen Deignan (Notre Dame, IN: Sorin Books, 2003), 19.

motives must be deep and our convictions clear. Nothing less can empower and sustain us.

. . . .

Questions to Ponder about **Faith:**

Examine your heart for the role "sacredness" plays in your worldview and motivations for creation care. How does your Christian faith strengthen and sustain you? How does it distract and disable you?

_____

_____

_____

_____

_____

_____

. . . .

One of the greatest difficulties of the environmental crisis is the temptation to burnout and despair. The problems seem overwhelming, and the human condition seems intractable. We can exhaust ourselves, emotionally and spiritually, swimming against that tide. These environmental challenges are enormous, and to sustain ourselves, we need to move forward not only in willful determination but also in hope for the work of God in the world. If we begin to believe that the world's future relies solely on our human effort and political will, we will lose sight of the hope that is at the center of our faith and fall prey to burnout. Despair and anxiety are not sustainable, and the pastoral teaching calls us to celebrate the grace that lies at the heart of a hope-filled celebration of God's whole creation.

This recognition of grace is key because of the overwhelming "to-do" list these challenges bring to our hearts and minds. Monk and theologian Thomas Merton wrote:

> There is a pervasive form of contemporary violence to which an idealist fighting for peace by nonviolent means most easily succumbs—activism and overwork. The rush and pressure of modern life are a form, perhaps the most common form, of its innate violence. To allow oneself to be carried away by a multitude of conflicting concerns, to surrender to too many demands, to commit oneself to too many projects, to want to help everyone is to succumb to violence. More than that, it is cooperation in violence. The frenzy of the activists neutralizes their work for peace. It destroys their own inner capacity for peace. It destroys the fruitfulness of their work because it kills the inner wisdom, which makes their work fruitful.[4]

. . . .

Questions to Ponder about **Motivation:**

As you have read about, listened to, or participated in environmental issues or actions, what motives for response and action were called upon? What was the long-term result?

_____

_____

_____

_____

_____

---

4. Thomas Merton, *Conjectures of a Guilty Bystander* (New York: Doubleday Religion, 1965), 81.

The heart of our response to the pastoral teaching, then, is not to rise up in an anxious rush to save the planet, but rather to order our lives to serve the Lord of Creation in faithfulness and love. This distinction is important, for it encourages faithful action, not frenzied activity and exhaustion. At the root of our motivation is not guilt, fear, or even indignation, but rather a song of praise and redemption. That which sustains our commitment and will to action is the joy of a fellowship with all living things, and the abiding conviction that God is present and working throughout all creation.

In so believing, we join in the song of redemption for all the earth, and sing that song not only with our voices, but also with our hearts and hands. We are being called to serve as Christ's hands and hearts in a hurting world, reaching out in love and rejoicing in God's grace. We do these things with the whole living body of Christ as it reaches toward hope.

As you consider what concrete actions you can take, do so with this prayer in your heart:

> May God give us the grace to heed the warnings of Jeremiah and to accept the gracious invitation of the incarnate Word to live, in, with, and through him, a life of grace for the whole world, that thereby all the earth may be restored and humanity filled with hope. *Amen.*

At the beginning of these sessions, you were invited to think of you own journey of care for creation, and reflect upon what ways your Christian faith has helped or hindered your commitment, using the chart on the next page. Revisit that question again. Have your answers changed? What do you need to do to strengthen the role of your faith in this journey?

HELPFUL	HINDRANCE
_____	_____
_____	_____
_____	_____
_____	_____
_____	_____
_____	_____
_____	_____

After the Session: Graceful Living

During the session, the group was invited to consider specific actions that could be taken for each of the five areas for both the good of our souls and the good of the world. Of the items listed, which actions called to you personally? Which items called to the group as a whole?

Identify the top item that called to you personally, and commit to taking first steps toward acting on it this week.

Identify the top item that called to the group, and commit to supporting group members in their choice. Reach out this week with a word of encouragement or an offer of support.

Be sure to include a form of celebration after completing these five sessions and all the good heart, mind, and soul you have offered to God in this time. Be sure to give thanks and accept with contentment the life of grace that is in your world.

APPENDIX A

A Pastoral Teaching from the House of Bishops of the Episcopal Church

Quito, Ecuador, September 20, 2011

Section 1: A Time for Repentance and Renewal (Confessional)*

That the church recognize and respond to this call for confession, compassion, and attention to the present crisis of the earth, and identify ways to speak and act on behalf of God's good creation.

[1] We, your bishops, believe these words of Jeremiah describe these times and call us to repentance as we face the unfolding environmental crisis of the earth:

How long will the land mourn, and the grass of every field wither? For the wickedness of those who live in it the animals and the birds are swept away, and because people said, "He is blind to our ways." (Jer. 12:4)

[2] The mounting urgency of our environmental crisis challenges us at this time to confess "our self-indulgent appetites and ways," "our waste and pollution of God's creation," and "our lack of concern for those who come after us" (Ash Wednesday Liturgy, Book

---

* Paragraph numbering, section headers, and summaries were provided by the authors.

of Common Prayer, p. 268). It also challenges us to amend our lives and to work for environmental justice and for more environmentally sustainable practices.

[3] Christians cannot be indifferent to global warming, pollution, natural resource depletion, species extinctions, and habitat destruction, all of which threaten life on our planet. Because so many of these threats are driven by greed, we must also actively seek to create more compassionate and sustainable economies that support the well-being of all God's creation.

[4] We are especially called to pay heed to the suffering of the earth. The Anglican Communion Environmental Network calls to mind the dire consequences our environment faces: "We know that . . . we are now demanding more than [the earth] is able to provide. Science confirms what we already know: our human footprint is changing the face of the earth and because we come from the earth, it is changing us too. We are engaged in the process of destroying our very being. If we cannot live in harmony with the earth, we will not live in harmony with one another."[1]

[5] This is the appointed time for all God's children to work for the common goal of renewing the earth as a hospitable abode for the flourishing of all life. We are called to speak and act on behalf of God's good creation.

Section 2: A Time for Grace for the Whole World (Sacramental)

That the church recognize that God's grace and plan for redemption encompasses all creation and to commit to embracing the whole creation as fellow recipients of grace.

[6] Looking back to the creation accounts in Genesis, we see God's creation was "very good," providing all that humans would need for abundant, peaceful life. In creating the world God's loving concern extended to the whole of it, not just to humans. And

the scope of God's redemptive love in Christ is equally broad: The Word became incarnate in Christ not just for our sake, but for the salvation of the whole world. In the book of Revelation we read that God will restore the goodness and completeness of creation in the "New Jerusalem." Within this new city, God renews and redeems the natural world rather than obliterating it. We now live in that time between God's creation of this good world and its final redemption: "The whole creation has been groaning in labor pains until now; and not only the creation, but we ourselves, who have the first fruits of the Spirit, groan inwardly while we wait for . . . the redemption of our bodies" (Rom. 8:22–3).

[7] Affirming the biblical witness to God's abiding and all-encompassing love for creation, we recognize that we cannot separate ourselves as humans from the rest of the created order. The creation story itself presents the interdependence of all God's creatures in their wonderful diversity and fragility, and in their need of protection from dangers of many kinds. This is why the church prays regularly for the peace of the whole world, for seasonable weather and an abundance of the fruits of the earth, for a just sharing of resources, and for the safety of all who suffer. This includes our partner creatures: animals, birds, and fish who are being killed or made sick by the long-term effects of deforestation, oil spills, and a host of other ways in which we intentionally and unintentionally destroy or poison their habitat.

Section 3: A Time for Justice and Sustainability (Prophetic)

That the church make connections between life choices and the corresponding participation in systems of injustice toward all neighbors, and examine ways to live into more sustainable ways of living and more just ways of praying, worshiping, fellowshipping, and serving.

[8] One of the most dangerous and daunting challenges we face is global climate change. This is, at least in part, a direct result of our burning of fossil fuels. Such human activities could raise worldwide average temperatures by three to eleven degrees Fahrenheit in this century. Rising average temperatures are already wreaking environmental havoc, and, if unchecked, portend devastating consequences for every aspect of life on earth.

[9] The church has always had as one of its priorities a concern for the poor and the suffering. Therefore, we need not agree on the fundamental causes of human devastation of the environment, or on what standard of living will allow sustainable development, or on the roots of poverty in any particular culture, in order to work to minimize the impact of climate change. It is the poor and the disadvantaged who suffer most from callous environmental irresponsibility. Poverty is both a local and a global reality. A healthy economy depends absolutely on a healthy environment.

[10] The wealthier nations whose industries have exploited the environment, and who are now calling for developing nations to reduce their impact on the environment, seem to have forgotten that those who consume most of the world's resources also have contributed the most pollution to the world's rivers and oceans, have stripped the world's forests of healing trees, have destroyed both numerous species and their habitats, and have added the most poison to the earth's atmosphere. We cannot avoid the conclusion that our irresponsible industrial production and consumption-driven economy lie at the heart of the current environmental crisis.

[11] Privileged Christians in our present global context need to move from a culture of consumerism to a culture of conservation and sharing. The challenge is to examine one's own participation in ecologically destructive habits. Our churches must become places where we have honest debates about, and are encouraged to live into, more sustainable ways of living. God calls us to die to old ways

of thinking and living and be raised to new life with renewed hearts and minds.

[12] Although many issues divide us as people of faith, unprecedented ecumenical and interfaith cooperation is engaging the concern to protect our planet. And yet, efforts to stop environmental degradation must not be simply imposed from above. Those most affected must have a hand in shaping decisions. For example, we welcome efforts in the United States to involve Native American tribal leaders and to empower local community organizations to address environmental issues. Similar strategies need to be employed in myriad communities in various locales.

Section 4: A Time to Renew Ancient Practices (Holiness)

That the church identify paths for healing from the Church's ancient traditions of fasting, Sabbath-keeping, and mindfulness and to apply them to local lives and churches.

[13] Our current environmental challenges call us to ongoing forms of repentance: we must turn ourselves around, and come to think, feel, and act in new ways. Ancient wisdom and spiritual disciplines from our faith offer deep resources to help address this environmental crisis. Time-honored practices of fasting, Sabbath-keeping, and Christ-centered mindfulness bear particular promise for our time.

[14] Fasting disciplines and heals our wayward desires and appetites, calling us to balance our individual needs with God's will for the whole world. In fasting we recognize that human hungers require more than filling the belly. In God alone are our desires finally fulfilled. Commended in the Book of Common Prayer, fasting is grounded in the practices of Israel, taught by Jesus, and sustained in Christian tradition. The ecological crisis extends and deepens the significance of such fasting as a form of self-denial: those who consume more than their fair share must learn to exercise self-restraint so that the whole community of creation might be sustained.

[15] Sabbath-keeping is rooted in the book of Genesis, where the seventh day is the day in which God, humans, and the rest of creation are in right relationship. In our broken world, keeping the Sabbath is a way of remembering and anticipating that world for which God created us. Sabbath requires rest, that we might remember our rightful place as God's creatures in relationship with every other creature of God. Such rest implicitly requires humans to live lightly on the face of the earth, neither to expend energy nor to consume it, not to work for gain alone, but to savor the grace and givenness of creation.

[16] The practice of Christ-centered mindfulness, that is, the habitual recollection of Christ, calls believers to a deepened awareness of the presence of God in their own lives, in other people, and in every aspect of the world around us. Such spiritual perception should make faithful people alert to the harmful effects of our lifestyles, attentive to our carbon footprint and to the dangers of overconsumption. It should make us profoundly aware of the gift of life and less prone to be ecologically irresponsible in our consumption and acquisition.

Section 5: A Time to Commit and Act (Behavioral)

That the church identify particular actions their local faith community can take in toward the areas of repentance, worship, stewardship, justice, and advocacy, and to commit to those actions.

[17] In assuming with new vigor our teaching office, we, your bishops, commit ourselves to a renewal of these spiritual practices in our own lives, and invite you to join us in this commitment for the good of our souls and the life of the world. Moreover, in order to honor the goodness and sacredness of God's creation, we, as brothers and sisters in Christ, commit ourselves and urge every Episcopalian:

- To acknowledge the urgency of the planetary crisis in which we find ourselves, and to repent of any and all acts of greed, overconsumption, and waste that have contributed to it;

- To lift up prayers in personal and public worship for environmental justice, for sustainable development, and for help in restoring right relations both among humankind and between humankind and the rest of creation;

- To take steps in our individual lives, and in community, public policy, business, and other forms of corporate decision-making, to practice environmental stewardship and justice, including (1) a commitment to energy conservation and the use of clean, renewable sources of energy; and (2) efforts to reduce, reuse, and recycle, and whenever possible to buy products made from recycled materials;

- To seek to understand and uproot the political, social, and economic causes of environmental destruction and abuse;[2]

- To advocate for a "fair, ambitious, and binding" climate treaty, and to work toward climate justice through reducing our own carbon footprint and advocating for those most negatively affected by climate change.

[18] May God give us the grace to heed the warnings of Jeremiah and to accept the gracious invitation of the incarnate Word to live, in, with, and through him, *a life of grace for the whole world*, that thereby all the earth may be restored and humanity filled with hope. Rejoicing in your works, O Lord, send us forth with your Spirit to renew the face of the earth, that the world may once again be filled with your good things: the trees watered abundantly, springs rushing between the hills in verdant valleys, all the earth made fruitful, your manifold creatures, birds, beasts, and humans, all quenching their thirst and receiving their nourishment from you once again in due season (Ps. 104).

[1] From *"The Hope We Share: A Vision for Copenhagen,"* a statement from the Anglican Communion Environmental Network in preparation for the United Nations Framework Convention on Climate Change (UNFCC), December 2009.

[2] We are indebted to the Episcopal Bishops of New England for their earlier 2003 Pastoral Letter, *"To Serve Christ in All Creation."* Several of these "commitments" and other phrases herein are quotations or adaptations of their work.

On the web:

Episcopal Church House of Bishops issues A Pastoral Teaching
www.episcopalchurch.org/posts/publicaffairs/episcopal-church-house-bishops-issues-pastoral-teaching-0

For more info contact:
Public Affairs Officer
The Episcopal Church
publicaffairs@episcopalchurch.org

APPENDIX B

Resources on Creation Care and Eco-Justice Concerns

Resources Available from Church Publishing: www.churchpublishing.org

- *Faith and Nature: The Divine Adventure of Life on Earth* by Phyllis Strupp is an eight-session, downloadable, intergenerational faith-formation resource focused on appreciating and living in harmony with God's creation.
- Michael Schut's books include an anthology of essays with community-building study guides:
  - *Simpler Living, Compassionate Life: A Christian Perspective*
  - *Food and Faith: Justice, Joy, and Daily Bread*
  - *Money and Faith: The Search for Enough*
- *To Serve and Guard the Earth: God's Creation Story and Our Environmental Concern* by Beth Bojarski is a practical parish or small-group resource suitable for high school groups and adults that connects the growing Christian environmental concern with the theology of creation in Genesis.

Worship and Prayer Resources

- *A New Zealand Prayer Book.* Auckland: The Anglican Church in Aotearoa, New Zealand and Polynesia, 1996.
- Rowthorn, Ann. *Feast of the Universe: An Interfaith Sourcebook of Ecological Spirituality from the World's Greatest Cultures and Religions.* Leeda, MA: Leader Resources, 2009.
- Rowthorn, Anne. *Feast of the Universe,* Leeda, MA: Leader Resources, 2010.
- Santmire, Paul. *Ritualizing Nature: Renewing Christian Liturgy in a Time of Crisis.* Minneapolis: Fortress Press, 2008.
- Stewart, Ben. *Watered Garden: Christian Worship and Earth's Ecology.* Minneapolis: Fortress Press, 2011.
- *The Green Bible.* New York: Harper Collins, 2008.
- *The Green Bible Devotional.* New York: Harper Collins, 2009.
- Wirzba, Norman and Fred Bahnson. *Making Peace with the Land.* Downers Grove, Illinois: Intervarsity Press, 2012.
- www.letallcreationpraise.org
- www.seasonofcreation.org

Faith and Ecology Books

- Bahnson, Fred and Norman Wirzba. *Making Peace with the Land.* Downers Grove, Illinois: InterVarsity Press, 2012.
- Berry, Thomas. *The Sacred Universe: Earth, Spirituality, and Religion in the Twenty-First Century.* New York: Columbia University Press, 2009.
- Bouma-Prediger, Steven. *For the Beauty of the Earth: A Christian Vision for Creation Care.* Grand Rapids: Baker Academic, 2001.
- Delio, Ilia, et al. *Care for Creation: A Franciscan Spirituality of the Earth.* Cincinnati, Ohio: St. Anthony's Messenger, 2007.
- DeWitt Calvin. *Earth Wise: A Guide to Hopeful Creation Care.* Grand Rapids, Michigan: Faith Alive Christian Resources, 2011.

- Edwards, Denis. *Ecology at the Heart of Faith: The Change of Heart that Leads to a New Way of Living on Earth.* Maryknoll, NY: Orbis Books, 2008.
- Grim, John and Mary Evelyn Tucker. *Ecology and Religion (Foundations of Contemporary Environmental Studies Series),* Washington, DC: Island Press, 2014.
- Horrell, David. *The Bible and the Environment: Towards a Critical Ecological Biblical Theology.* London: Equinox Publishing, 2010.
- MacDuff, Mallory, *Sacred Acts: How Churches are Working to Save the Earth's Climate.* Gabriola Island, British Columbia: New Society Publishers, 2014.
- Macy, Joanna and Molly Young Brown. *Coming Back to Life: Practices to Reconnect Our Lives, Our World.* Gabriola Island, British Columbia: New Society Publishers, 1998.
- McKibben, Bill. *Eaarth.* New York: Henry Holt and Company, 2010.
- Mosely, Lyndsay. *Holy Ground: A Gathering of Voices on Caring for Creation.* San Francisco: Sierra Club Books, 2008.
- Santmire, Paul, et al. *God's Earth is Sacred: Essays on Eco-Justices.* National Council of Churches Eco-Justice Program, December 14, 2011.
- Swimme, Brian and Mary Evelyn Tucker. *Journey of the Universe.* New Haven: Yale University Press, 2011.
- Torgerson, Mark. *Greening Spaces for Worship and Ministry: Congregations, Their Buildings, and Creation Care.* Durham, NC: Alban Institute, 2012.
- Tull, Patricia K. *Inhabiting Eden: Christians, the Bible, and the Ecological Crisis.* Louisville, KY: Westminster John Knox, 2013.

Environmental Justice Resources

- WEACT—www.weact.org (NYC)
- Urban Habitat—www.urbanhabitat.org (Oakland)
- Delco Alliance for EJ—www.ejnet.org/chester (Philadelphia)

- Little Village Environmental Justice Organization—
  www.lvejo.org (Chicago)
- Deep South Center for Environmental Justice—
  www.dscej.org/ (Louisiana)

General Info about Gardening, Agriculture, and Fair Trade Coffee

- Biodynamic Farming and Gardening Association:
  www.biodynamics.com
- The USDA's Sustainable Agriculture Research and Education
  Program: www.sare.org
- Local Harvest: www.localharvest.org/csa/
- Bishops Blend: www.er-d.org/BishopsBlend/
  (a collaboration with ERD and Pura Vida Coffee)

Networks and Organizations

- Blessed Tomorrow: www.blessedtomorrow.org
- Earth Ministry: www.earthministry.org
- Episcopal Church Foundation, Vital Practices,
  www.episcopalfoundation.org/
- GreenFaith: www.greenfaith.org
- Interfaith Power and Light: www.theregenerationproject.org
- The Episcopal Ecological Network: www.eenonline.org
- The Episcopal Network for Economic Justice: www.enej.org
- The Episcopal Public Policy Network: www.episcopalchurch.org/
  eppn.htm
- The link to the "Getting Started on the Genesis Covenant" resource
  guide: www.episcopalchurch.org/sites/default/files/genesis_
  convenant_final.pdf
- Web of Creation: www.webofcreation.org
- Yale Forum on Religion and Ecology: fore.yale.edu/